Copyright © 2018 by JMosley Publishing
All rights reserved. This book or any portion thereof may not be reproduced or used in any manner whatsoever without the express written permission of the publisher except for the use of brief quotations in a book review.

Printed in the United States of America

Table of Contents

Dedication 4
Introduction 6
Overview 9
The Story 13
REFLECT 15
Day 1 Why Have I Chosen To Mentally Detox At This Time? 18
Day 2 Who Am I? 21
Day 3 How Am I Doing? 24
Day 4 What Are The Causes For Each Emotion That I Most Frequently Feel? 27
Day 5 How Do I Usually Deal With Difficult Emotions Or Situations That Occur In My Life? 30
Day 6 How Do I Take Care Of Me? 33
Day 7 What Are The Barriers To Me Taking Care Of Me? 36
RELEASE 39
Day 8 Release Negative Thoughts And Concerns In A Journal 42
Day 9 Release Some Emotional Energy 45
Day 10 Address An Issue 48
Day 11 Engage In A Stress Releasing/ Coping Activity 52
Day 12 Identify Individuals, Situations And Bad Habits That You Plan To Let Go 55

Day 13 Release What Does Not Make Sense 59
Day 14 Write A Letter Of Release 63
RESET/ REFOCUS 66
Day 15 Live In The Moment 69
Day 16 Shift 72
Day 17 Change/ Improve Your Routine 75
Day 18 Establish Emotional Awareness 79
Day 19 Establish A Self-Care Regimen 82
Day 20 Plan Your Next Break Or Vacation 85
Day 21 Establish Mental Wellness Goals To Hold Yourself Accountable 88
REPLENISH 92
Day 22 Think Positively, Speak Positively 94
Day 23 Show Gratitude 97
Day 24 Utilize Supports 100
Day 25 Improve Your Diet 104
Day 26 Utilize Exercise 108
Day 27 Be Social 111
Day 28 Disconnect 114
Review/ Refine 118
Day 29 Review Progress 119
Day 30 Refine Results & Goals 122
Day 31 Commit To Wellness 125
Prayer 130
Let's Stay Connected! 131

Dedication

All glory and honor to God, for allowing me to achieve my childhood dream! Thank you for the purpose you have assigned to my life, even when I don't understand it. There is none like you!

To my amazing husband and children, I love you all so much! I am so thankful to you for supporting me through another venture! The love, understanding and encouragement you give is indescribable. You all are THE BEST!

To my parents, thank you for always believing in me and encouraging me to follow my dreams from childhood to adulthood. I love you! To each brilliant lady who picks up this book…You are amazing! Remember that! Success and blessings to you!

The Mental Detox

By Dr. Valeka Moore

Introduction

Hello beautiful! What an amazingly brilliant woman you are! You are a leader in business, education, church, media, government, military or in your community. You are a role model, maybe a wife, or a mother, a caregiver, possibly a entrepreneur or an executive, maybe even a student in higher education preparing for the next level in your career or the mastermind getting things done behind the scenes. Whew! Regardless of your role or likely numerous roles, I think it is safe to say you were created for greatness! God created you as his masterpiece (Ephesians 2:10) and has called you to a phenomenal purpose. However, even the amazingly brilliant masterminds get tired, overwhelmed, feels defeated, unappreciated or just flat out knocked down and dragged out by life at times. Although for many women, even in those tough moments, we muster up the energy and strength to refresh our lipstick, reposition our crowns and straighten out our capes, while maintaining our poised appearance and our roles of being THE EVERYTHING to everyone. We surely managed to live by Philippians 4:13 (NKJV), "I can do all things through Christ who strengthens me." We put our emotions and needs to the side to accommodate others and to keep things moving, because things just cannot function without us. Right? "I'll just deal with it later." "I'll set time aside for me later." Me, me, me.... Later, later, later. However, often times *later* takes weeks, months, or even years to show up. Take a moment to think, when was the last time your later became your *NOW*. With all of the brilliance we hold as women, we just cannot seem to figure out that one thing.... the formula for proper self- care. But listen ladies!

The absolute real of it is that EVERYTHING begins in and with our minds. As God has blessed us with this powerful tool to imagine, dream, create think on and embrace the beauties and wonders of life, He also knows that our minds take in those things that are contrary. Therefore, the word of God instructs us to renew our minds Romans (12:2). This is advice not to be taken lightly, and we should be mindful to implement as often as possible.

Life presents us with distractions, unfavorable circumstances, challenges, hardships and devastation, which over time, can build up and weigh us down. If we do not take time to care for our mental and emotional health needs, roots become planted or residue is left behind, that will sometimes attempt to consume our well-being. Those roots and residue are mental toxins, which causes us to become burdened, feel sick, remain tired and prevents us from living a truly mentally balanced, happy and healthy life. And when we are not mentally balanced, nothing in our life is truly stable or able to flourish.

It is important to me, that incredible women like you, around the world, achieve optimal levels of mental wellness and functioning. I often experience many well-meaning coaches, encouraging individuals to make shifts in their mindsets, by thinking differently, in order to live a more positive life. While I do agree with this notion, I know that it is almost impossible to make such mental shifts when: 1) We do not know how to even begin shifting our mindsets and 2) Our minds are filled with so much clutter and dysfunction. What I have often found with clients and personally, is that because of the clutter and dysfunction that takes up space in our minds, there is very little room for new information and cognitions to enter and effectively penetrate. Therefore, minimal change ever occurs. That is why it is necessary to first detox and clear any blockage that would prevent one from embracing new thoughts and undergoing mental shifting.

Woman leader, you have been called to something great, so it is imperative that your mind be as free and clear, as possible, of what is not benefitting! Every single day you are taking in new and wonderful information that motivates you to keep dreaming up new ideas, pursuing new passions, sharing more and serving more. However, the bible tells us that we cannot pour new wine into old wineskins (Matthew 9:10). Therefore, you cannot effectively absorb, embrace and activate the brilliance that the Father has purposed for you, if your mind is so crowded and stretched to the brim with stress, chaos and confusion. Lovely lady, brilliant woman, it is time for a MENTAL DETOX.

Overview

A very important part of maintaining positive mental health is becoming and remaining aware of specific mental and emotional factors that specifically impact you on a regular basis. This book will guide you through a 31day journey of mental detoxifying activities, which target various mental wellness components, specific to the woman leader. Every seven days you will enter a new phase of the detox, totaling four phases, followed by a review. As you begin each phase there will be a description of and information to coach you through the process of that phase. You will receive insight regarding why each phase, along with each step is important, and how to effectively implement the strategies for best results.

This Mental Detox is for women looking to rid themselves of toxins such as lingering stress, anxiety, and any thoughts and feelings that may interfere with their overall functioning, which is currently or could potentially prevent them from successfully achieving the life that they want and deserve. The detox is especially beneficial for those preparing for a personal life transition or starting a new chapter in their life. It will also be useful for those getting ready to begin a process or any situation that requires clarity and focus.

The Mental Detox will provide you strategies utilizing 5 R's (Reflect, Release, Reset/ Refocus and Replenish) to assist you in recognizing and eliminating and cleansing toxicities in your mind, followed by shifting and restoring your mind with clarity, focus, productivity, fresh and positive feelings, thoughts and perspectives for the optimal functioning you desire. . Commitment to the process and full engagement is vital to your detox efficiency. Your detox success will depend upon your openness, your engagement and your commitment to the process. One important thing to note is that the Mental Detox is not a fix all-cure all.

You may need to either complete the detox again, sooner or later (I suggest at least once per year) or take additional steps after the detox (ie: counseling or coaching). However, there will be work for you to do, even if it only consists of continuing to implement strategies in order to maintain the progress obtained. A part of being committed and engaged in the process is being open and honest. That is the only way you will be able to truly get in touch with what needs to stay, what needs to go and what you need to add. Just a disclaimer, you may not always like what you find or how it makes you feel, but push through the discomfort. It's a vital part of the process. Also, do not be discouraged if you do not complete the detox within 31 days. You may find that some of the tasks require more thought or work than can be thoroughly implemented in one day. There is no need to rush. Transformation requires diligence and focus.

Take a moment and identify personal or professional supports that will hold you accountable but will also be there for you to contact, for encouragement and comfort, in case things become too challenging. If you foresee any challenges, speak to your accountability person to brainstorm how you may be able to make this work best for you. You are encouraged to incorporate faith-based principles and strategies to keep you spiritually fueled for the journey. So, feel free to utilize prayer, your bible, affirmations and gospel or inspirational music, in addition to the content in this book.

Now, I know you are ready to be free and clear, but before diving in head first, I want to make sure you are fully prepared to take on this transformative endeavor. The more prepared you are, the more likely you are to remain consistent and experience a successful completion.

Here are a few tips to help you get ready:
-Plan a day to begin. The 1st day of the month or Sundays or

Mondays are recommended days to begin.

-Begin in the morning. Although you may not be able to thoroughly complete the activities in the morning, it is important to take a few moments to read the content for that day, shortly after you have awakened, so that you know how to set your focus, for the particular day.

-Specify some downtime to be able to fully engage in the activities each day. At least 30 minutes per day is encouraged.

-Identify a peaceful, quiet room or space with very limited distractions, that others rarely occupy. Or let others know that you will need privacy and quiet for a specified amount of time.

-Get plenty of rest on days leading up to the detox and throughout the detox

Things that you may want to utilize during the detox:

-A new journal specifically for the detox. Here you will record responses to the questions presented within each exercise (if needed), progress and barriers, notes from accountability talks with your support system and anything else you would like to document pertaining to the detox. There is also space at the end of each day's activity, where you can record notes and personal observations.

-At least one support person to hold you accountable to complete the detox

-Bible, affirmation book or other positive reading content

-Items that help calm and relax you (i.e.: herbal teas, candles, aromatherapy items, music, etc.).

-Healthy and concentration enhancing food items (i.e.: fish, whole grains, leafy greens, lean protein, yogurt, nuts, berries, dark chocolate, etc.)

Things you should limit/ eliminate during the detox
-Stressful/ negative people
-Stressful/ negative situations
-Negative, maladaptive and self -harming behaviors

Oh, one more thing ladies… Take off those capes, the crowns and definitely the masks. It's time to get real with YOU.

Once you have removed all of the enhancements and stripped down to flaws and all, but most importantly the wonderful masterpiece that God designed decades ago, you are now ready to go on this journey. I am so excited about the work you will do and the new freedom and wellness that you will achieve! Be blessed!

The Story

One day in late 2013, a woman sat quietly at her desk, at her place of employment. Her desk was filled with papers, apparent of tasks needing to be completed. She felt burned out, worn down, frustrated, worried, overwhelmed and a mound of other disturbing emotions. However, her job was not the cause of this mountain of emotions that she felt (well maybe in part), but her feelings were coming from places much deeper. The cares of life, that she had pushed down, way down to the depths of her very soul. She could barely concentrate on anything positive or necessary, such as family time with her loving husband and beautiful children or the dream business that she would finally be starting, in the next few months. The wonderful things in her life, were now overshadowed by stressors, negativities, burdens and concerns that she held sacred. On that day she felt old. She felt as though she was aging by the minute. She was drained and could literally feel strength...no, life being sucked from her body. She felt like she was dying. Of course, it sounds bad, but for her, it felt even worse. The more that she tried to keep contained the uninvited thoughts and feelings that she had been carrying around for years and had kept tightly concealed, they were erupting right in her very mind and being released throughout her being.

"It was never meant for you to carry" kept ringing in her head. Those were the words spoken to her by a preacher who had visited her church to minister, months before. "It was never meant for you to carry."

And on that day, the strong, determined, ambitious, subservient young woman knew she could not go another year living life the same way. Something had to change. Plenty had to change. And it had to start in her mind. A real transformation needed to take place mentally. It was time for a detox. A cleansing. A release. No, it wasn't always easy and no it didn't always feel good, but she had to let some things go. In order to be the best wife, mom, daughter, friend, minister, therapist, coach, entrepreneur, but most of all the best version of herself. The masterpiece that God had created her to be, she had to release some things. Did I mention that woman was ME? Yes, I have been there. Now it's your turn. Because, it was never meant for you to carry.

REFLECT

Brilliant Woman Leader!

Welcome to WEEK ONE and the first phase of the *Mental Detox*. This step consists of fully recognizing and understanding the reason why it is important for you to detox at this time. You cannot successfully complete the journey if you do not understand the value in taking it. You may not be aware of all of the underlying toxins that need to be released through the detox, however you have an understanding that there are some areas that cleansing and elimination need to take place. In this detox YOU will be your primary focus.

Therefore, self-reflection will be an integral part of this process. And for the next seven days you will reflect and reflect and reflect some more.

In order to engage in self-reflection, it is important that you understand the concept of reflecting. Reflecting causes, you to obtain deeper insight than what is normally seen or easily accessible. In a nutshell, self-reflection is a process that simply consists of you connecting with you. Connecting with your thoughts, your feelings and your actions. Now, take a moment to complete an honest assessment regarding how frequent you actually self-reflect. Think about how often you really take time to connect with yourself. It is so easy to get lost in what is going on around us that we can go weeks, months even years without taking time to reconnect with ourselves and truly consider the who, what, when, why and how's of our innermost being. It is important that we find time to regularly connect with ourselves by disconnecting from the world and our surroundings, in order to evaluate how we really feel. I already know what you are thinking.

"She cannot possibly be talking about me." "Disconnect?" "I'm just too busy." "My family needs me." "My children need me." "Work needs me." "There is just no time for me." Trust me, I get it. I have been there. But guess what? You cannot go on like that forever. When you fail to connect with you and care for you, you lose you under piles of everyone else's needs, wants, schedules, agendas and the weight of everyone else's baggage. You lose you in the busy-ness, the distractions, the hardships and even the celebrations. I promise it is perfectly OK for you to disconnect and take care of you for a while or from time to time. Definitely more often than what you do now. You are not being selfish. You are not being mean. Everyone will be fine. There is no need to feel guilty. Caring for you will make you better for you and everyone else. If you do not take time for you, you WILL get worn down and burned out. Then how will you take care of everyone and everything? Even better question, *who will take care of you*? Believe me when I say "You Are Well Worth It." Now, *reflect* on that.

Day 1
Why Have I Chosen To Mentally Detox At This Time?

Good Morning Brilliant Woman Leader,

Welcome to day 1! I know you were probably hoping for a much more dramatic first day activity. However, it is that simple. There is a reason why you have chosen to undergo this process. From the time you decided to purchase this book, there was something inside of you that let you know it was time. What was it? What was your why? Why do you need this? Your why is what will keep you focused and persistent during the next 31 days. Although you may not be fully aware of every single toxin, you know that there is something that needs to be eliminated. There is something that you do not want to carry any longer. Or maybe you just want to complete a mental self-check. A *mental wellness check-up*, I like to call it. That is great! Whatever your reason, it is important that you know where you are and what you want to achieve. Having an awareness of these aspects now, will be vital to your productivity throughout this detox and you being able to effectively measure your success at the end.

Day 2
Who Am I?

Good Morning Brilliant Woman Leader,

Do you remember the dream life you had planned out in your head, twenty, ten or one year ago? Has it come to fruition? Have some parts manifested? Or does your current life resemble an entire different life than you planned? Even someone else's life perhaps? Are you happy or even content with the outcome of your life and the role you play in it? Have you gotten lost in it, somewhere along the way? You may be feeling discontent. You may be feeling like you are living the life someone else wanted for you. You may even feel overjoyed about how your life has turned out and still find yourself feeling consumed and often disconnected from your own self. If you fail to take a moment periodically, to slow down, check where you are, evaluate your growth or lack thereof, and assess where you're headed, you may begin to feel completely out of touch with YOU.

Today you will reflect on who YOU are at the present time. Consider what YOU want for your life. Compare and contrast who you are and what you wanted for your life 10, 5 and 1 year ago, with who you are and what you want now.

Day 3
How Am I Doing?

Good Morning Brilliant Woman Leader,

Today you will take a moment to simply stop and ask yourself, "How am I doing?" Simple enough, right? But guess what? FINE is not an acceptable answer. It is time to be completely honest. I know you do not ask yourself this often and you may answer quite superficially when asked by others. However, have you ever experienced a situation in which you had just had enough? You were tired of biting your tongue. You were done with being nice or being understanding. It was time that *they* knew how you really felt. Well my dear, this is your "Let me tell you how I really feel" moment. But this time, the person who you are telling is YOU.

Identify 3-5 emotions that best describe how you most frequently feel. Because we usually do not think past 4 surface emotions (happy, sad, angry, frustrated).

I have included a copy of a detailed emotion chart in *The Mental Detox Experience* Facebook group. Feel free to use this chart or another emotion identification resource to dig deep. Freely and specifically identify the particular emotions that you experience most regularly.

Day 4
What Are The Causes For Each Emotion That I Most Frequently Feel?

Good Morning Brilliant Woman Leader,

On day 3, you identified 3-5 emotion words that you feel most consistently in your life. Today you will dig even deeper and face a new reality relating to your emotions. In today's task you will identify and reflect on the separate causes of each of those emotions. Think about which situations, activities or individuals, in your life, cause you to feel each particular emotion? Why do they cause you to feel that way? Complete this activity for both the positive and unfavorable emotions you have identified.

Day 5
How Do I Usually Deal With Difficult Emotions Or Situations That Occur In My Life?

Good Morning Brilliant Woman Leader,

Over the past two days you have identified the emotions that you most frequently experience, as well as the people and situations that are attached to those feelings. Today you will reflect on how you manage situations and emotions that are difficult for you. Consider how you handle tough situations that happen daily (ie: working at a stressful job, rushing through traffic to take children to extracurricular activities, etc.) or even situations that occur from time to time. Remember those emotions you identified on day 2? Think about what you do with those on a daily basis. Identify a recent situation or emotion that you have had to manage. Also evaluate a past situation(s) or feeling(s) in which you are still dealing with the effects. Identify positive as well as maladaptive coping mechanisms that you utilize.

Day 6
How Do I Take Care Of Me?

Good Morning Brilliant Woman Leader,

Take a moment and breathe. Take another deep breath and let it out slowly. I think today is a great day to reflect on self-care. Often when we consider self-care, we tend to think about the physical health aspects of care. We may change our diet, exercise or lose weight. As women leaders we may even focus heavily on our appearances (hair, nails, skin, attire, etc.). While these elements of self-care are important and may even make you feel great and should be included in your self-care plan, always remember, it is equally necessary to target mental health self-care. This consists of doing things just for you, not only because you need to, but because you really want to. Mental health necessities, such as taking a break, saying "no" at times or any change to other's normal expectations of your role, sometimes come with a great deal of guilt or anxiety. With your busy life of caring for everyone's needs and everything else along the way, how do you take care of yourself? Think about exactly what you do. When do you do it? How often? Do you ever take time just for you?

Day 7
What Are The Barriers To Me Taking Care Of Me?

Good Morning Brilliant Woman Leader,

Yesterday you were encouraged, maybe even challenged, with identifying ways that you take care of yourself. How did that go? Don't be hard on yourself if you came up a little short or with nothing at all. Trust me we will remedy that soon. The resolution is generally revealed once we pinpoint the barriers.

Today you will identify and reflect on the thoughts, feelings, people and situations that have hindered you from properly caring for you. The only way for you to begin to take better care of yourself, is to understand the barriers that have kept you from doing so, in the first place.

RELEASE

Brilliant Woman Leader!

Welcome to WEEK TWO! You did it! You made it through an entire week of reflecting. What a great job you have done thus far! How are you feeling as a result of self-reflecting? What did you learn about yourself?

Sometimes reflecting is not easy. If you feel mentally drained, overwhelmed, restless or any other unsettled emotion, these are normal reactions to the process. You may have observed the surfacing of difficult or painful feelings that you had forgotten about or did not even realize were there, because you have been so busy with life or have simply tried to distract yourself. You may have found it hard to relax or even sleep last week, due to allowing yourself to dig deep and bring up all of the thoughts and feelings that have been ignored and tucked away. The exposure of those cognitions and emotions were necessary, in order for you to effectively move through this next phase. Although we may not always want to, we *need* to feel our emotions.

They are the mental apparatus, which helps us remember that we are human. Otherwise we would keep going and going and going, like robots. Repeat after me, "I am not a robot." We are supposed to feel our emotions. They alert us to stress and other mental toxins that break down our mental/ emotional health. Whether you have been carrying the mental toxins around for hours or years, it is important to acquire knowledge for properly managing our emotional states and dealing with stress and other mental toxins.

In this next phase of *Release,* you will recall the thoughts, feelings, behaviors and people that you identified in the *Reflect* phase and determine what should be purged or eliminated. Daily we encounter people and situations that cause mental toxins to be unleashed in our minds. Over the next seven days you will be guided through techniques to help you properly decrease or eliminate those toxicities, which is also known as de-stressing or decreasing stress. Decreasing stress helps you to cope better and improves your mood, causing you to feel happier, more optimistic and overall better.

It is important to understand that we each have unique ways of effectively coping, de-stressing and ultimately releasing. Pay close attention to determine the most successful strategies for you.

On a side note, remember you cannot take on the emotional baggage of others either. But I digress.
Let's continue...

Day 8
Release Negative Thoughts And Concerns In A Journal

Good Morning Brilliant Woman Leader,

Over the past week you have done a lot of work! Today you will REST YOUR MIND.

Use your journal to release any strong, persistent or lingering thoughts and worries from last week's exercises. Especially before you go to bed. Deal with them tomorrow. Repeat this exercise for the remainder of your journey, if needed.

Day 9

Release Some Emotional Energy

Good Morning Brilliant Woman Leader,

How was your mental rest? On Day 8 you were encouraged to rest and leave any difficult thoughts and concerns to be cared for today. It is important to know that we should not constantly carry around stress. Although it is a normal tendency for us to resist or bury our emotions, it is not a natural process to keep them inside. When we hold stress in or even push it down deep within, it does not evaporate, dry up or go away. It is remains and is destructive to our minds and bodies, sometimes causing an onset of mental and/ or physical illness. And brilliant woman you have so many amazing things ahead, that you have absolutely no time for what can be avoided.

So, let's get to work. Take some time today to release built up or lingering emotional energy. Allow yourself to feel the emotions that go along with past and present stressful concerns and situations. Send the children outside. Send the husband to the store for milk. Send the employees home for the day. Or just go for a drive. And for you ladies who have subconsciously picked up your capes and crowns, this is your reminder to replace them on the shelf... Now let loose. Scream, cry, yell! It's OK. Just get it out! Repeat as needed.

Day 10
Address An Issue

Good Morning Brilliant Woman Leader,

Whew! How did it feel to let it out?! Do you feel a little lighter today? A little freer? That's wonderful! Let's keep that momentum going! Take some time today to get some things off your chest...or actually off your mind. At times we will put tasks off because of inconvenience or lack of motivation. Or we will attempt to avoid situations that make us feel uncomfortable, uncertain or like we are overreacting. Leaving things alone or sweeping them under the rug can feel easier when we are just trying to keep things moving forward, other aspects of our lives seem priority or we are trying to avoid conflict. However, we still reflect on these unaddressed tasks and situations from time to time or a great deal of the time. They become distractions and sometimes even consume a significant amount of mental space, causing limitations to our capacity to function in other tasks and other areas of our lives. You know that situation or concern that you have tried to ignore or the comment that person made the other day that you tried to let slide?

Today, address at least one of those challenging issues in your life. After all woman leader, one thing you are known for or getting better at is stepping out of a comfort zone. Well here is your chance. No longer allow those pesky thoughts to consume your mind, with should've, could've, would've or "I wonder." Go ahead and go for that promotion, begin preparing for that relocation, move on from that relationship (personal or professional), fill out that application, finish writing that book (Hello! Sometimes, I need to speak to myself).

If it's a conversation that needs to happen, initiate and

facilitate it. It does not have to be aggressive, but definitely be assertive. Think about what it is that you want to say and the information you wish to receive and deliver. Lastly, even if that issue is something as simple a paying or setting up a payment plan for a bill, completing a task at work or something you have been saying that you are going to do, like clean out the junk drawer, deal with it now to reduce stress in the future.

[50]

Day 11
Engage In A Stress Releasing/Coping Activity

Good Morning Brilliant Woman Leader,

Yesterday's activity was designed to release you from an unaddressed stressful situation. However, it is very possible that it evoked some sudden stress before, during, after or in all of the above, as you anticipated the outcome or actually completed your task of addressing the issue. What did you do to manage that stress? Anything? What positive strategies do you currently utilize to manage day –to- day stressors in your life? A couple days ago you enjoyed a good cry. The reality is that most of us do not cry daily or close to it, nor feel the need to release in that manner. However, it is vital that we still manage normal day- to day stressors, by utilizing positive coping strategies.

Today you will identify at least one or two stress-relieving activities and put them to practice. If you can, try both a high energy (ie: exercise, kick-boxing, running, dancing, etc.) and a low energy (ie: stretching, deep breathing, journaling, painting, etc.) activity. Evaluate their effectiveness in boosting your mood or making you feel relaxed. Continue to try other activities during the remainder of the detox, in order to secure those that work best for you. Also consider coping techniques that can be appropriately applied in numerous settings and to various situations (ie; home, work, social situations, etc.)

Day 12
Identify Individuals, Situations And Bad Habits That You Plan To Let Go

Good Morning Brilliant Woman Leader,

On Day 11, you worked on identifying positive stress relieving activities, also known as coping mechanisms. Over the past few days you have also engaged in various tasks that will help you manage and release stress, moving forward. Utilizing those strategies will help you avoid the buildup of stress, however it is important that you eliminate or limit those things that cause you stress in the first place.

Based upon your observations during week one, you have become more aware of the individuals and situations that cause you stress and other emotional harm.

Sure, you may not completely remove a parent, child or other close relative from your life, but can you limit your interaction, if it is stressful or damaging to you? Can you change the way you interact with them? You also noted maladaptive behaviors or bad habits (ie: self-limiting talk, allowing people to dump their emotions or problems on you, allowing verbal abuse, co-dependence or over dependence on others, assuming the role of a victim, etc.) and maladaptive ways of coping (ie: holding in emotions, over-eating, overspending, drinking more than usual, isolating, etc.) that you may engage, that then escalates that stress and emotional harm. Which individuals, situations or bad habits have you realized the need to release or reduce from your life? Now, which of those identified do you actually plan to let go? This is the million-dollar question, which could hold a life changing outcome if you would just release them. Journal your responses. What are your reasons for not releasing that one or those few individuals, situations or habits? What stressful thoughts or emotions surface as a result of you considering to release them. Consider the purpose that the situation or person is serving in your life, for you to continuously hold on to such situations. What do you think or even fear will happen if you let it go? What thoughts or emotions surface as a result of you choosing to not release them at this time? Woman leader, I encourage you to weigh your feelings in the moment, to the probability of emotions that you will continue to experience in six months, one year, five years or longer, if the situation goes unchanged. Is giving in to your current feelings of guilt, shame or fear, worth missing out on the peace and freedom that will come with the change? Hmm Definitely something to ponder. But I encourage you to take some time to get still and pray for guidance here, especially when it comes to individuals. Definitely seek clarity who, when and how, to help you move forward with peace assurance.

Day 13
Release What Does Not Make Sense

Good Morning Brilliant Woman Leader,

On Day 10, we focused on addressing an issue. Hopefully you were able to address or make a plan for addressing many situations which you may desire an answer. However, if you found yourself still unable to let something go, after addressing those issues, there are likely underlying reasons that this has been difficult.

A lot of our mental space and emotional energy is consumed by thoughts pertaining to why something that we do not understand has happened to us. "How could she do that to me? I was always there for her. I don't understand. I just need to know why."

Why did that traumatic situation happen to me? My life was going just fine. I did everything I was supposed to do. It doesn't make sense. I need answers." Can you relate?

Sometimes we can spend years or a lifetime waiting to receive answers to questions, which we will never receive. Either the person to provide the answer will never be truly honest with us or we are not satisfied with the responses that we do receive. Or sometimes the individual is no longer alive or in a competent state of mind to give us answers. Another, possibility is that there was no actual person that caused us hurt or harm. We may never get what we think we need. A viable explanation. An honest heartfelt apology.

And if we do accomplish these responses, it may still be less than enough. It is important that we allow ourselves freedom from those situations which we have not been able to attain comprehension. We have to find acceptance in not receiving *the right* answers. Acceptance does not mean that you have to agree with the wrongdoing, or that you like it or it feels good. The acceptance is facing the reality that the offense or situation occurred and that the explanation, apology or lack thereof is what we have. We will need to accept even the things that do not make sense, or we will never be able to find peace and move forward.

Today, write down any situations that have occurred in your life that you have been unable to make sense of, regardless of your efforts. Try to identify the reasons that you have been unable to obtain understanding, answers or feel settled with what you have received? What else do you think that you may need, in order to find fulfillment in this area? Do you believe you will ever be able to achieve what you are seeking? Are you willing to work toward acceptance?

Day 14
Write A Letter Of Release

Good Morning Brilliant Woman Leader,

Yesterday, you identified the individuals, situations and bad habits that you need/ plan to release. Today, you will write a good-bye letter(s) to the individuals, situations or bad habits that you actually plan to release now. It will be up to you whether you actually mail or give the letter to the individuals they were written to. These letters are meant to serve as a tangible reminder of your release from these various aspects of your life. For extra accountability, you can seal the letter(s) in a self-addressed envelope and give to an accountability partner to hold on in case you ever encounter challenges with follow through. There is nothing like your own inspirational words to get you back on track. Next, because some changes in our lives require steps, develop your step-by-step strategy for releasing those individuals, situations or bad habits. Imagine them out of your life or limited from your life. How does it feel?

RESET/ REFOCUS

Brilliant Woman Leader!

You have made it to WEEK THREE! Excellent job! Now breathe... And breathe again...

I know *Release* week was a bit of an emotional roller coaster. One day things were calm and the next you were challenged to take some steps that may have evoked some uncertainty, discomfort and mental preparation. Nevertheless, you made it through and this week you really do get to breathe. Really. So go ahead and completely exhale.

Now that the negative people and situations are gone or at least limited, you have created some valuable mental space. I recently heard a fellow wellness expert say "When we release we reset." This week you will learn and implement strategies to help you mentally reset and refocus. So often, we go and go and go and go. Our bodies go. Our minds go. And we rarely take a mental break. This causes mental blocks, mental baggage, mental overload and more. And eventually we become mentally stuck. Stuck in a mindset that is resistant to the need to make changes or improvements. At this point we need to move away from a *mindset* and undergo a *mind-shift*. Resetting is all about making the necessary shifts for proper positioning. Once positioning occurs, we are able to hit the reset button and prepare for what is ahead. Refocusing is all about putting things in proper perspective. This concept is just like using a camera. If a camera is not properly focused the picture will appear blurry or distorted. The camera may need to be refocused in order to sufficiently view all that it is meant to capture. There are certain experiences throughout our lives that play a larger part in how we adapt to and survive in the world around us. We formulate certain ideas by listening to the perspectives of those close to us and observing their behaviors, during our youth.

We adopt certain patterns and operate in particular facets, due to our fears, doubts, disappointments and the limits imposed on us by others. Usually because we tend to be set in our ways, wounded by life or so busy pursuing life or trying to survive it, we opt to maintain our perspectives and beliefs, because they seem to be what works best. Perhaps we could look at things differently, but we have to be open Now that you have taken time to release, you have made room to allow new information and ideas to effectively penetrate. At this point you will be able to see things as they are and take action. Over the next couple weeks begin to think about some of those of things that you have wanted to do, how they will impact your life and you outlook on the future. It's time to get aligned and focused so that you can magnetize all the beauty and positivity that God has for your life.

Day 15
Live In The Moment

Good Morning Brilliant Woman Leader,

With so many distractions around us and always so much to do or be concerned about, we seldom fully experience the world around us. Today simply focus on being in the moment...living in the moment. Be intentional about focusing on what you are doing. Try to cut out multitasking and anything that disrupts your concentration on the thing that is priority at that time.

Slow down and be mindful of the beautiful intricacies surrounding you in your usual environment and in nature. Eat lunch outside. Pay attention to the design of your community. Feel the breeze on you face. Watch the waves at the beach. Pay attention to how the leaves blow in the light wind. Throughout the day take a few mental breaks. Taking opportunities to be in the moment causes us to feel alive and give attention to what really matters in life. These opportunities also allow us to gain awareness regarding how we truly feel and what we need, to be able to shift and refocus at that time. Take opportunities today, at least five minutes at a time, to take deep breaths and give consideration to how you are doing in the moment. Consider what you need at that very moment. Complete this about 3 times throughout the day.

Day 16
Shift

Good Morning Brilliant Woman Leader,

In order to effectively reset, sometimes the things around you need to change in order for proper shifts to take place in your mind. Now of course we do not have direct control over everything, but what about the many simplicities in life that you are able to easily change or improve? What simple shifts need to take place in your life right now? What things needs to be organized? Cleaning, restructuring or even slightly adding to a room or a work space or a closet can help you mentally shift. Clear off your desk, change the location of the couch, add a plant or fresh flowers. You will feel more organized and have more clarity.

Is it time for a change of environment? A permanent or temporary move? A vacation or stay-cation perhaps? Is it time for a new place of employment or a new work position? Do you need to improve the way you care for yourself physically? Do you need to eat healthier, exercise more, get more rest? Do you need to be more spontaneous? When was the last time you went and got a massage? Sat on the porch? Spent time with friends? Make at least one small shift in your life today. Plan for the others moving forward.

Day 17
Change/ Improve Your Routine

Good Morning Brilliant Woman Leader,

Another essential step to mentally refocusing/ resetting is changing or improving our daily routines. We are significantly more productive when we establish an organized way of living. The first essential piece of a daily routine is how we start our day. Do you have a relaxed morning routine, or is it unorganized and chaotic? Consider starting your day in quiet and stillness, with devotion, meditation, stretching or simply breathing deeply. Yes, it may require you to wake up a bit earlier, but the peaceful tranquility, will be well worth it. Just five minutes could impact the flow of your entire day. Imagine opening your eyes to serene stillness rather than stressful texts or emails alerting you of the urgent matter you will have to deal with at the office. Imagine waking up and not immediately having to jump into mommy mode, yelling for the children to wake up, and of course having to call them numerous more times when they don't actually get up, or reminding them to brush their teeth or to stop hogging the bathroom mirror. Need I say more?

Do you take mental breaks and lunch breaks throughout the day or do you sit at your desk for hours or never stop running errands, because you do not want to get behind in your work? The mid-day reset is also quite essential. Guess what? You are actually less productive when you do not incorporate breaks. Step away from your work. Take a walk. Sit outside of a café' with your favorite drink. Breathe in fresh air. When you have been working as incredibly hard as you have (remember almost having to drag your precious child out of bed or taking your husband that big report that he forgot at home and desperately needed for work, all before getting to the office to de-escalate that crisis), you deserve a break.

Now, how about the end of the day? Does your day ever end? Do you have a bed time? Yes, an actual time scheduled to lie down, close your eyes and drift off in a deep slumber? No television. No reading. No work. If you answered "no" you are definitely not alone. Most busy ladies do not have a set bedtime. Although a bedtime is a highly recommended way of acquiring the rest that we need, I understand it may not always work out this way. However, do you have a way to properly unwind before bed? This is crucial. An evening routine alerts both, our minds and bodies that we are winding down for the evening. It will help you sleep better throughout the night and feel more rested in the morning. Do you have at least 30 minutes to an hour of down time prior to preparing to sleep? Your routine can include a shower or a bubble bath, aromatherapy, a cup of herbal tea and/or any mindless activity (an activity that you enjoy, which requires very little focus or thought and naturally soothes and relaxes you), such as, meditating, praying, journaling, watching television, reading, scrolling social media (my favorite for bedtime is Pinterest), listening to relaxing music or even exercise or stretching. Develop and begin implementing your new routines today.

Day 18
Establish Emotional Awareness

Good Morning Brilliant Woman Leader,

How was your evening and certainly how are you feeling this morning? A restful sleep and a calm morning can bring mental clarity like you would not believe, which makes today the perfect day to establish emotional awareness. In order to properly reset you have to be clear regarding your need to reset. It is important to understand the effects that stressful situations, busy schedules, draining or negative people and all the cares of life have on our emotional state and functioning. Do you know your emotional baseline? This is your calmest state. How do you know when you are calm? How do you know when you are leaving your calm or peaceful state? What begins to happen? Do your palms sweat? Does your heart race? Does your face turn red or pale? Then what do you do? Bite your nails? Pace back and forth? Become argumentative? Become quiet?

Take some time throughout the day to pause and think about how you are feeling. Take note of how it feels when you are absolutely calm. Be mindful of how you feel when other emotions arise. Even the positive ones. Certain emotions may present different physiological responses.

Additionally, consider your overall mental-emotional well-being. When are you at your emotional best? How do you feel during those times? What is typically going on or not taking place in your life? Take a moment to measure your current well-being. On a scale 1-10 (10 being your best), where are you right now? Identify what do you need or need to do, in order to be at a 10 or at least two points higher than you are currently?

Day 19
Establish A Self-Care Regimen

Good Morning Brilliant Woman Leader,

Earlier in the detox, we established that self-care is an important and necessary part of maintaining mental wellness. You have reflected on the self-care activities you presently incorporate into your life and any hindrances to engaging in self-care.

Now, it's time to figure out what you are going to implement on a regular basis, to ensure that you are sufficiently caring for YOU. Identify at least three self-care activities that you will intentionally incorporate into your lifestyle (relaxing, massage, bubble bath, going out with friends, getting more sleep, going to hairdresser, ordering takeout one evening each week instead of cooking, etc.). Engage in at least one self-care activity today.

Day 20
Plan Your Next Break Or Vacation

Good Morning Brilliant Woman Leader,

Looking at the same things, talking to same people and completing the same tasks daily, can become mundane and zap you of your emotional and physical energy. Every now and then, it is time for a change of scenery and/ or a change of pace, which helps you to not only reset but also recharge. When was the last time you took a trip or a full-on vacation, unassociated with work and children?

Today you will plan your next vacation! Where will you go? When? How long? Go on that dream vacation, or that place you have been considering for a while, or even visit with friend or relatives out of town. If you can go this weekend or next week, excellent! But try to schedule your vacation for a timeframe within the next 3-6 months. You will have something to look forward to, that will not be far from reach. Trips and vacations that are a weekend or more are great! However, if you are only able to take a day trip or overnight, that is perfectly fine as well. But just get away!

I do realize that this may be harder for some than others because the first step for you is actually taking a day from work. If this is you, plan at least 3 days away from work. Even if you just choose to remain home on a stay-cation, it will be a nice change of pace, to just experience life without being at the office. And no work of any kind allowed. You deserve it!

Day 21
Establish Mental Wellness Goals To Hold Yourself Accountable

Good Morning Brilliant Woman Leader,

    A lot in our lives, we just work on getting done. Not always because we want to, but because we have to or are expected to. We do not generally set goals to tasks. We women leaders just get things done! Or if we do apply goals, they pertain to our physical health, our finances or our professional goals. Rarely ever do we set goals to target mental wellness. Over the past few weeks you have reflected on how you are really feeling and the emotional toxins that you have picked up along the way, which have become a part of your being. You have worked toward releasing those mental toxins and finally resetting and focusing on areas of your life that you can change or improve, in order to achieve increased mental wellness. For the past few days, you have been encouraged to view your surroundings and mental health needs through a new lens and at different angles, then the views you have held to closely to over time.

    Today you will establish mental wellness goals for moving forward. These goals can be taken from the needs you have identified or the routines and regimens that you have created this week. Make sure your goals are specific, measurable, attainable, realistic and timely.

    And most of all, be honest. If there is something that you do not see yourself doing, right now, save it for later. Goals can always be updated. Evaluate and update your progress after the first 30 days and then every 90 days, thereafter.

Examples

<u>Goal 1:</u> I will engage in better self-care, evidence by taking 30 minutes, at least 3 days per week to be by myself and relax by journaling and listening to relaxing music.

<u>Goal 2:</u> I will maintain emotional clarity, evidenced by taking lunch breaks for at least 20 minutes per day, away from my office.

<u>Goal 3:</u> I will rest 2 nights per week evidenced by writing my worries or task for tomorrow in my journal and leaving my thoughts there until 7am in the morning. I will also be in bed by11pm on those two nights.

These are just examples. You will complete your goals based upon what your identified needs. You can have more than one goal in a particular area. Try to have no more than 3-5 goals at a time, to avoid becoming overwhelmed. When you achieve one goal you can add another. Choose your goals by determining what areas are priority or what goals may also target and help you achieve success in other areas.

REPLENISH

Brilliant Woman Leader!

WELCOME TO WEEK FOUR and the final phase of the Mental Detox!!! Are you still hanging in there with me? I assure you, it is all leveled ground from here. Smooth sailing. Perhaps this detox has felt everlasting or maybe it has flown by. Whatever your experience, the key is that it has been transformative to your life and mental wellness journey. I believe now is a great time to complete a review to remind you how far you have come. During the first week you completed self-reflection and really got in touch with your inner most emotions. In the second week you learned about releasing mental toxins and worked to release toxins such as individuals, situations and bad habits, that have a negative or stressful impact on your life and emotional state. Last week you took time to reset and refocus, to ensure that you were correctly positioned, with a clear view of the things that are healthy to your mind and your life, helping you to maintain productivity and remain positive.

Now that you have cleared mental space and properly reset, new and affirmative information can now effectively penetrate your mind. It is vital to refill your mind this way, otherwise the same toxic substances will re-accumulate. This week is all about restoring, replacing and filling up mentally, with what is healthy. The key to effectively replenishing is to begin with putting in the right substances, that will build you up, make you strong and sustain you for the long run. When you were younger, your parents insisted that you eat your vegetables, so that you would grow big and strong! Same concept here. Let's replenish!

Day 22
Think Positively, Speak Positively

Good Morning Brilliant Woman Leader,

As a woman leader, you are likely thinking non-stop (except when you are sleeping so restfully ☺) and speaking into the lives of others on an ongoing basis. You are continuously pouring out, and even taking in, which is why it is necessary that you strengthen your mind daily. You have to feed and nurture it with the right matter. The words that we say, see, hear and have a very powerful impact on our mental well-being. That is why we have to be clear on what we need and do not need to say, see and hear. Words can build us up or tear us down. A couple weeks ago you considered the who's and what's that caused certain emotions and decided on which ones needed to be released or limited, as much as possible. Remember, we have choices regarding what we allow in. And we have to speak life daily. Today take some time to locate and write down a few bible verses, affirmations and positive thoughts that you can see, speak and hear each day. Start your morning off with these. Say them throughout the day. Put them in areas that you enter throughout the day, so you can see them. Make a recording of you or someone else reciting them for the days you feel you do not have enough strength to recite them yourself. Say, see and hear even if you don't feel it. Trust me you will eventually begin to believe them.

Day 23
Show Gratitude

Good Morning Brilliant Woman Leader,

Are you feeling grateful today? It is a wonderful day to show gratitude! Yesterday you were assigned to write down some scriptures, affirmations, thoughts, etc. that help you to feel peaceful and positive.

It's important to for you to begin your day positively and to end positively. It is also important to be aware of how the thoughts that you have in the first 17 seconds of waking up can shape your day. Today you will continue to focus on thinking positively. Surely everything may not be as we would like it, however we ALWAYS have something to be grateful for. The more we focus on being grateful the less impact our ever changing and sometimes undesirable circumstances have over us.

Being mindful of what's going well or what we appreciate in our lives helps us to be strengthened and more peaceful when we deal with difficulties. Take some time today to get still and focus on the who's and the what's and certainly don't forget about the whys. The WHY gives meaning and substance to our gratitude. Write at least ten things that you are grateful for and the reasons behind your gratefulness.

Day 24
Utilize Supports

Good Morning Brilliant Woman Leader,

Support is a very important aspect of human living and can come in many forms. Regardless of the type of support, simply having and utilizing support helps us to stay emotionally grounded. There is nothing like having someone call when you need a listening ear. Or having someone to help you figure out provision when you need something. Or simply someone to say an encouraging or kind word, give you a hug, hold you accountable or let you know that they are there for you. A couple weeks ago you identified individuals who may not have been beneficial to your emotional health and that you may have needed to limit or cease interaction. Today you will think of those who positively impact your life. Those who are there when you need them and do not mind being there for you. Understand that having a support system is vital to your emotional wellness. Brilliant woman leader, yes you are strong and have great ability to function independently, nonetheless statements such as "I don't need anyone" "I don't have anyone" cannot remain acceptable reasons for choosing to not utilize a support system.

Truly we all need someone sometimes. Often, we feel that we do not have support because we feel uncomfortable or guilty about reaching out to others and possibly burdening them or we feel as though no one will truly understand. Other times we expect others to read our minds regarding the support we need and when and how we need it. Unfortunately, those thoughts and mindsets leave us completely unsupported. Remember we all need support at some point. You are not the only one and you don't have to be alone. Write down the name of those individuals who you deem supportive and how they positively impact or influence your life. What value do they add? Remember, no two supports are exactly alike. Identify how you will continue to utilize each support in your life. For example, who can you ask for a cup of sugar? A small loan? A ride to the store? A listening ear? Prayer? Encouragement? Accountability? Etc.

Day 25

Improve Your Diet

Good Morning Brilliant Woman Leader,

Did you know that your diet is just important to your mental health as it is to your physical health? A healthy diet helps balance mood and decrease stress. Particular foods can decrease symptoms of anxiety or depression, while others stimulate those symptoms.

Additionally, a lack of concentration and memory deficits can result from a poor diet, where a good diet can improve concentration and memory.

Some helpful suggestions for items to limit include caffeine and sugar, amongst others. Can you guess which types of foods are good for you? A few includes nuts, fish, fresh fruit, fresh vegetables, whole grains, etc. Additionally, it is important that you stay properly hydrated by doing plenty water throughout the day.

When we encounter stress, our bodies become dehydrate and when we are dehydrated, we are more prone to stress. Additionally, be sure that breakfast is incorporated into your diet. Breakfast helps to fuel your brain as well as your body and can help prevent symptoms of fatigue and increase mental clarity.

Today you will adjust your diet. Research foods to see what are helpful to your mental as well as physical health and which are harmful? What are some foods or substances that you need to add in your diet? What are some food or substance you need to remove or cut down on? Do you skip meals? Do you eat proportionate meals? Do you drink enough water? Do you take any vitamins or supplements? Plan your meals and be mindful of what you eat today. Consider systems such as weekly meal prepping or preparing meals the day before to ensure a more healthy and balanced diet. Make plans to target all of these areas. Be realistic in your goal planning. Not everything has to be implemented at once, however develop your plan of action for the next month.

Also, consider consulting a certified nutritionist or dietician that specializes in diets plans that target mental wellness.

Day 26

Utilize Exercise

Good Morning Brilliant Woman Leader,

Whether it is for health, enjoyment or you have a weight loss goal to accomplish, we understand that exercise, just as our diets, is important to the physical and mental health areas of our lives. Our brains produce endorphins, which helps elevate our mood.

When we exercise, more endorphins are released and as a result we feel happier and symptoms of stress and depression are reduced and confidence is improved.

Walking, running, swimming, dancing, bike riding and sports are only a few examples of exercise that you can engage. Today is a lovely day to get out and engage in some form of exercise. Choose an exercise that you can do for at least 15-30 minutes. Woman leader I know that you may already be quite active, keeping up with work and the children, however you still need another form of exercise. Take some time to write down an exercise schedule to continue, even if it is only for a couple days per week or a few minutes per day.

Day 27
Be Social

Good Morning Brilliant Woman Leader,

What are your plans for today? Will you spend time with girlfriends? Attend a concert or festival? Go to lunch with coworkers? A conference or networking event? Sit on the porch and chat with neighbors? There is no better day than today to get out and socialize! It is wonderful to catch up with friends and loved ones that we have not seen for a while. It is also fun to get out and meet new people. I know this may require a bit more energy for my fellow introverts but go ahead and step out of your comfort zone.

Stepping out of comfort zones is something the woman leader knows how to do very well. Being social can lift our spirits, strengthen our relationships, give us energy and increases our productivity. It also keeps us emotionally connected and sheds light and gives us new perspectives regarding the things that are happening in our lives. The right balance of social activity will improve our mental and physical energy and decrease stress. Enjoy a day of connecting with others and being social!

Day 28

Disconnect

Good Morning Brilliant Woman Leader,

    I hope everyone enjoyed a day of getting out and socializing. Spending time with family and friends and/ or meeting new people. Although it can feel great to get out and be social, sometimes it can leave us feeling tired, drained or completely wiped out. Every so often, it is great for us to be able to just disconnect, be alone and do absolutely nothing. It is stated that two days of disconnecting and doing little to nothing, can leave us feeling like new people. I encourage everyone to eventually schedule some time to take two full days or longer to disconnect. However, for today, I encourage you to take at least 2 hours (sleep time does not count) to completely disconnect, from people (yes that includes the children), work, the to do list, social media, things that cause stress, etc. Stay in your room, go somewhere else isolated, walk a trail, sit out on a pier, etc. To some this may seem unimaginable. For others, this may feel uncomfortable. "What will I do for two hours or two days all alone, without doing and thinking about my regular stuff?" This is exactly the point! This will be a great time to get acquainted with you. Take time to observe who you have become or are becoming. Time to be at ease with you and not worried about validation form others. Allow the Holy Spirit to speak to you clearly, give your insight and direction and provide comfort regarding the things concerning you. This is a time Learn what you enjoy. Do something that you have been wishing to do for a while (read that new book, listen to the music you enjoy, pray, draw, binge watch a new television series, craft, garden, etc.). Or do absolutely nothing. Just breathe and enjoy! If you are unable to make time to complete this today, plan for a day and time in the next few days. Trust me, it will be absolutely exhilarating!

Review/ Refine

Brilliant Woman Leader!

Can you believe you are nearing the end of the detox?! You have done so well! These next few days are all about making sure you feel comfortable with the tools you have been provided and the activities that you have carried out over the past few weeks, so that you are able to effectively maintain them in your life and continue positive mental wellness.

It's now time to review, refine and commit.

Day 29
Review Progress

Good Morning Brilliant Woman Leader,

Today you will review the progress you have made throughout the mental detox. And darling, believe me, you have made progress. You may not be exactly where you want to be or where you thought you would be but take a few moments to reflect on where you were prior to beginning the detox. I assure you are not in the same mental space. Always remember, it is about progress and not perfection. Keep going and you will get there. Start over and do it again. It is OK.

You will get there. Now, go back, beginning with day one. Do you feel that you have properly or thoroughly completed the exercises for each day? If not take about an hour today, to go back and complete any tasks not given thorough attention or write down your plan for completion, by day 31 or within the next week. Also think about the progress you have made. Think about what tasks or weeks were most helpful to you. Consider what you have enjoyed about the detox. Think about what was most challenging. Think about what emotional/ mental areas you feel you are still struggling. Consider what components of the detox may be difficult for you to continue to carry out. Write down your responses to each of these reflections.

Day 30
Refine Results & Goals

Good Morning Brilliant Woman Leader,

I hope you were able to take some time to review your progress, decide what possibly needed some additional time or effort and to make plans to sufficiently complete.

Today you will review the responses you provided yesterday, regarding what has gone well and what areas require additional progress. Additionally, take a moment to remember your response to the task on Day 1, "Why have I chosen to Mentally Detox at this time?". Did you achieve your desired result? What results were not achieved? What hindered you from achieving those results? With regard to the goals that you established a couple weeks ago, do you feel that they are specific and measurable enough for you to be able to continue to work toward and sufficiently monitor your progress? Also, at this time, consider reaching out to your accountability person, a coach or a therapist, to provide you with feedback and support, with refining your goals and obtaining the results you are seeking.

Day 31
Commit To Wellness

Good Morning Brilliant Woman Leader,

    IT'S DAY 31!!!!!!! Congratulations to you for hanging in there! You have done an excellent job! I know that some days may have been difficult and maybe you felt like stopping, but you persevered and kept pushing through, because of your determination to successfully complete this program and take control of your mental health!!! Now that you have taken this first step, to detox from the toxins and residue of past experiences, it is time for you to totally commit to your wellness. It is necessary that you continue to utilize the tools that you have received. Continue to make those investments in yourself. You deserve it. Today, you will Commit To Your Wellness. When I say Wellness, I mean every aspect of it. Remember they all work hand in hand. Take some time today to think about what you want for your health, moving forward.

    What will it take for you to successfully attain those things? To start it will take commitment. A couple weeks ago you established goals for yourself, however setting goals is useless if there is no commitment or accountability to reach them. Today, write a commitment to yourself for moving forward in your mental wellness journey. What do you commit to do? Why is it important to your life? How will you do this? Etc.

    Now take your commitment letter and put it somewhere safe. Pull it out after 30 days and read and evaluate. Continuously renew your commitment to yourself, at least twice per year, to evaluate your follow through and recommit if necessary.

Here are some additional suggestions for keeping your progress at the forefront of your mind:

1) Start a progress journal- Record the progress you continue to make. Even the small progress. Example: maybe you have never relaxed before and you take an evening to sit and do nothing that's progress. Example #2: You are always doing for others, but just need a day to yourself. Someone calls asking you to do something. You say "no." Your progress journal entries can connect to your goals or simply be about progress that you notice in yourself. It can also reflect feelings.

If you said that on most days you feel stress, worried or unsatisfied and you begin to feel peaceful, calm and content (even for a day) write that down, along with other any changes or contributors that made you feel that way.

2) Record backtracking behavior- and just as you record your progress, it is also important for you to record your steps backward.

This is a way to hold yourself accountable. Backtracking behaviors include falling back into old maladaptive patterns or even engaging in a maladaptive behavior just once. It is important to be mindful from the beginning. Example: you have set aside one day per week to relax. You do good for one month but then miss a week. What happened? What changes? Record that with the date of the step back and write your plan of action to get back on track. This should be a small section in your progress journal.

3) Select an accountability person- It should be someone who is really going to hold you accountable and not allow you to slack. Someone who can be honest with you. Let them know your goals and let them know how you would like them to hold you accountable. Also have a day set aside, maybe weekly or by weekly, to discuss your progress and what they have seen from you. This person should be someone that you communicate with regularly or will begin to communicate with regularly. If you have not

already, give consideration to working with a coach or therapist for 90 days to one year, or more, to support you with remaining engaged and accountable to your commitment.

Prayer

Father God!

I come before you, graciously thanking you for another day. What an incredibly amazing God you are! I thank you for each and every gift you have placed inside of me to touch and serve your precious women across the world. I thank you for the brilliant woman, who has just completed this mental detox. I pray that the content in this book has been a blessing to her mentally, physically and spiritually and that it significantly impacts her life in the weeks, months and years to come. We ask that you seal the clarity, healing and restoration that has taken place, like only You can. I thank You for the unique calling that you have divinely assigned to her life, as a bold and powerful leader. I thank You for the work she will continue to perform and the individuals she will continue to impact through her gift of leadership. Continue to order her steps and direct her path, Lord. Equip her with more strength, faith, love and joy for the journey. Wrap her in your peace that surpasses all understanding, to guard her heart and mind in Christ Jesus. Give her rest and send true support when she needs it God. Keep her protected from every attack that the enemy has planned, to disrupt or destroy her purpose. Cover her and continue to shine through her with your brilliant light. Lord, I love You and I praise You and give You all the glory and honor! In Jesus' mighty name I pray. AMEN!

Let's Stay Connected!

Brilliant Woman Leader!

Or can I call you girlfriend at this point? ☺ Over these past few weeks, we have been through a lot together It has been an absolute pleasure, taking you through this journey, as I also experienced it a few years ago, and time and time again, as I have moved forward as a successful woman leader. I would love stay in touch and learn about your experience, so that I can continue to make this program and follow up efforts, more successful, for those of you who read this book, as well as those who attend our groups and retreats around the world. I invite you to join *The Mental Detox Experience* community on Facebook, to interact with other Mental Detox participants. You will also receive updates regarding our upcoming events and new products. And please don't forget to leave your feedback and testimonials.

You can also connect with me on the following social media platforms:

Facebook: Dr. Valeka Moore-Speaker & Coach
Facebook: Dr-Valeka Moore
Instagram: drvalekamoore
LinkedIn: Dr. Valeka Moore
Website: www.valekamoore.com
Email: info@drvalekamoore.com